BUG
DETECTIVE

MAGGIE LI

Amazing facts, myths, and quirks of nature

STERLING CHILDREN'S BOOKS
New York

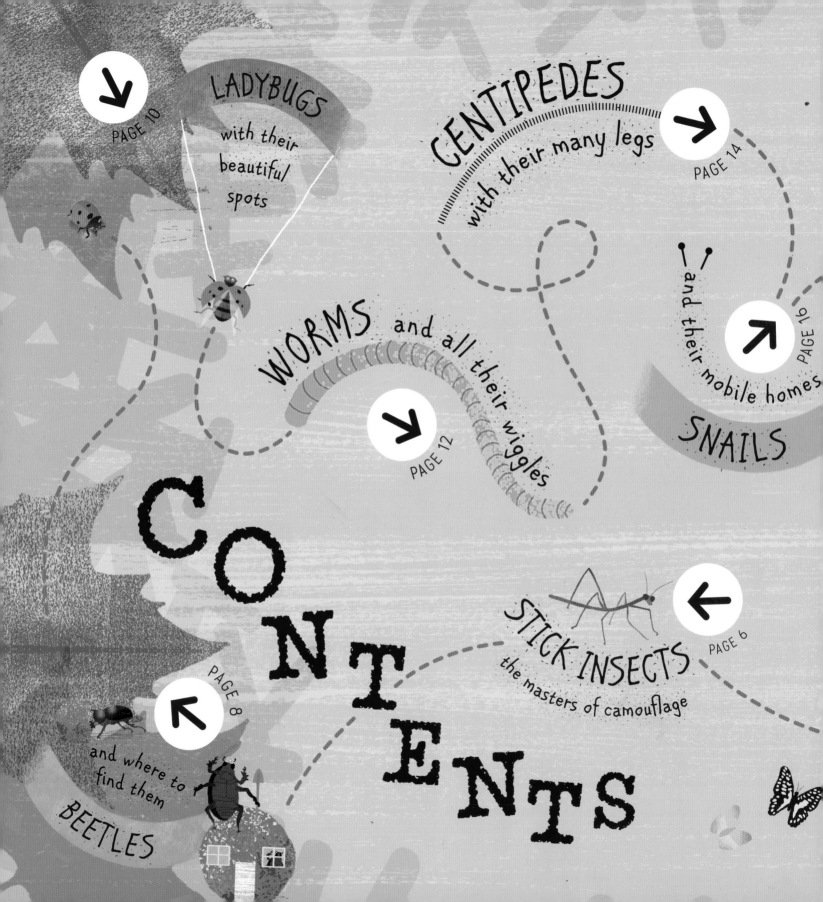

LADYBUGS with their beautiful spots
PAGE 10

CENTIPEDES with their many legs
PAGE 14

and their mobile homes
SNAILS
PAGE 16

WORMS and all their wiggles
PAGE 12

STICK INSECTS the masters of camouflage
PAGE 6

and where to find them
BEETLES
PAGE 8

CONTENTS

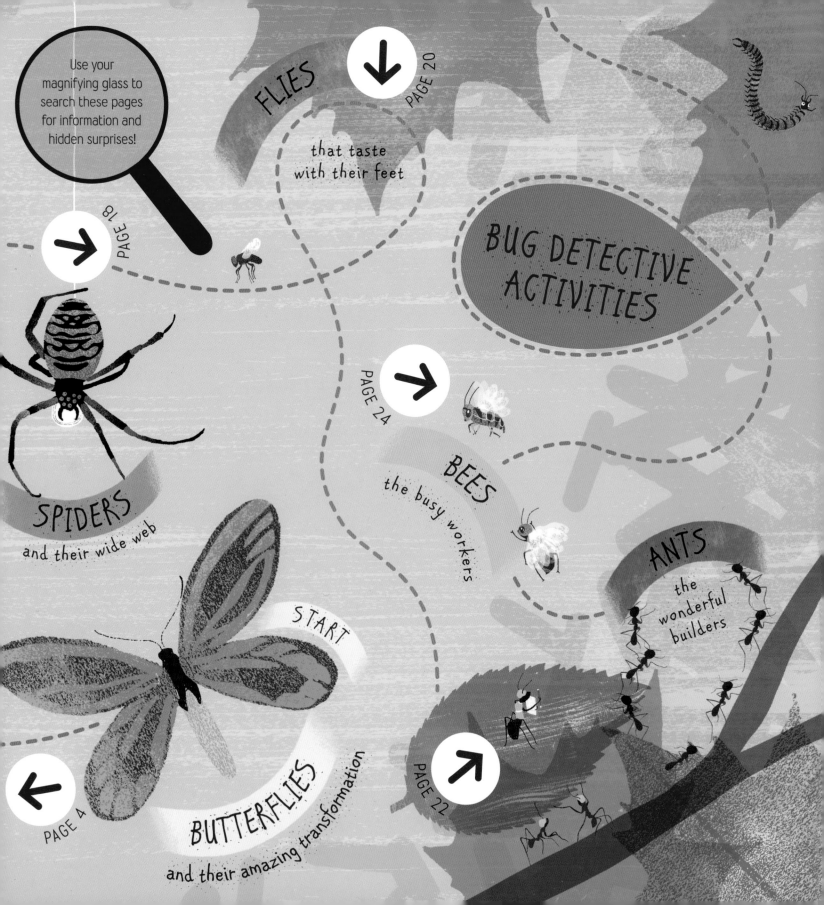

Use your magnifying glass to search these pages for information and hidden surprises!

FLIES
that taste with their feet

PAGE 20

PAGE 18

BUG DETECTIVE ACTIVITIES

PAGE 24

SPIDERS
and their wide web

BEES
the busy workers

ANTS
the wonderful builders

START

PAGE 4

BUTTERFLIES
and their amazing transformation

PAGE 22

Butterflies have to be careful of birds that like to snack on them!

MISSION

Some butterflies are camouflaged so they look like flowers. Can you spot all 18 butterflies on these pages?

4.
Inside the chrysalis the caterpillar is going through amazing changes . . .

CATERPILLAR SOUP

Its old body parts are turned into a kind of "soup," out of which the new butterfly parts are grown.

3.
When the caterpillar is fully grown it turns into a chrysalis.

1.
Butterflies start life as tiny caterpillars. A caterpillar has one and only one job, to eat!

MINI MUNCHERS

Burrrp

2.
Caterpillars eat so much and grow so quickly that they change out of their skins four or five times.

BUTTERFLIES

Butterflies are one of nature's most beautiful insects, but they start their life as caterpillars. They transform into butterflies through an amazing process called metamorphosis. Their short, fat bodies are replaced by long, slender legs and graceful, colorful wings. Imagine waking up one day and finding that you look completely different!

BIG AND SMALL

Butterflies come in all shapes and sizes.

The smallest known butterfly is the pygmy blue, which has a wingspan of less than ½ inch.

The biggest butterfly is the Queen Alexandra's birdwing, which can grow to up to 12 inches!

BIG CHANGE

BUTTERFLY FOOD

Butterflies don't eat, they drink! They have a long strawlike mouth, called a proboscis, which sucks up nectar.

Life Cycle

Eggs

Butterfly

Larva (Caterpillar)

Pupa (Chrysalis)

BUTTERFLY FEET

Butterflies don't taste with their tongues like we do, they taste with their feet.

Mmmm delicious!

How does this one taste to you?

SUNBATHING

Butterflies need warmth from the sun to help them fly, that's why we see them on sunny days.

MOST COLORFUL AWARD

Some stick insects are brilliantly colored or striped. Others have beautiful wings that they flash open and shut to startle predators.

DID YOU KNOW?

Have you ever wondered why they're so good at sticking to things? They have special suckers and claws on their feet so they can walk up walls and even upside down.

MISSION

Stick insects look so much like bits of plants that they blend into their background. See how many you can find hiding in the trees!

MOLTING MADNESS

After it molts a stick insect will sometimes eat its old skin!

Stick insects have lots of nifty ways of escaping predators. Some make a loud hissing noise using their wings.

ESCAPE ARTISTS

COPY CAT

By curling their tails over their backs, stick insects can trick predators into thinking they are scorpions.

LIQUID ATTACK

Some species can squirt a yucky liquid into their attacker's eyes, giving them time to run away.

Others will suddenly drop to the ground and play dead.

They can even shed the odd limb to escape an enemy's grasp!

STICK INSECTS

Stick insects are famously difficult to spot. Chances are you've probably come across quite a few and never noticed them! They normally live in tropical environments, but some species live near you. Their most impressive quality is their twiglike appearance, which helps them to hide from predators and prey!

The Chan's megastick from Borneo is a whopping 20 inches long, making it the longest insect in the world.

WORLD'S LONGEST

LEAF INSECTS

Some have flattened bodies and look more like leaves than sticks. Sometimes their disguise is so good that other insects start nibbling on them!

Life Cycle

Eggs

Nymph

Adult

A nymph sheds its skin as it grows

MYTH BUSTER

With its plantlike appearance, a praying mantis is often mistaken for a stick insect. It's not—it's a mantid. Mantids hunt and eat insects, while stick insects are happy munching on leaves and berries.

ANT BABYSITTERS

These masters of camouflage disguise their eggs to look like tiny seeds. Ants carry the eggs to their underground nests, eat the fatty end, and leave the rest of the egg in the nest where they hatch, safe from predators.

MATERNITY WARD ✚

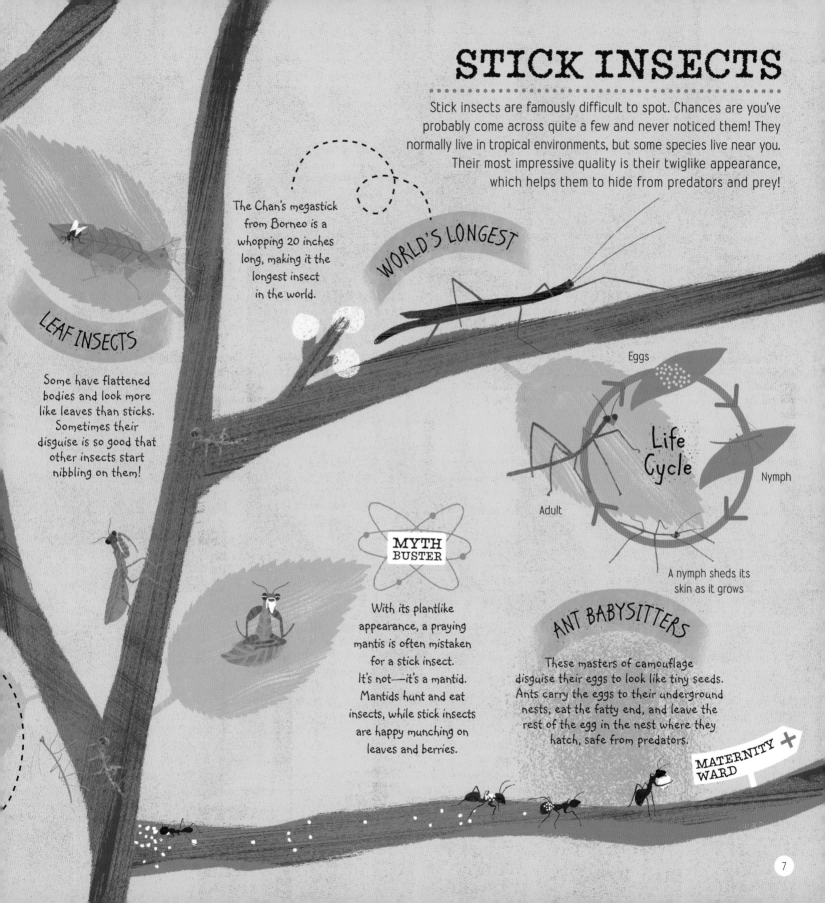

BEETLE GUIDE

There are 3 kinds of dung beetle:

Tunnelers   Rollers   Dwellers

But which one's which?

Can you match the beetles to their category?

DUNG HOME

Dung beetles sometimes make their homes out of poo!
Roller beetles roll the dung into a ball using their legs and head.
Dweller beetles just dive straight onto the dung and live there.

A dung beetle is so strong it can pull over 1,000 times its own body weight. That's like an average person pulling 6 double-decker buses!

Are we nearly there yet?

BIG BEETLES

The titan beetle can grow as big as nearly 6 inches and can snap a pencil in half with its enormous jaws.

DUNG BABIES

Dung beetles are nature's recycl they roll dung into balls that th eat later. Without them th earth woul be piled high wi manur

Dung beetles lay eggs in dung. Their babies hatch inside, then eat their way out of it.

NATURE'S RECYCLERS

BEETLES

There are more species of beetle than any other creature on the planet. They come in lots of different colors and sizes, and have some extraordinary talents. So get moving and see how many kinds you can find in your own garden or local woods.

Beetles come in all shapes and sizes, and include ladybugs, glow-worms, fireflies, and the long-necked giraffe weevil of Madagascar!

Auntie Dot   Grandma Glow   Cousin Wilbur

WE ARE FAMILY

Life Cycle

Eggs

Adult

Larva

Pupa

TUNNELING BEETLES

Tunneler dung beetles bury their dung in an underground network of tunnels.

Beetles have two sets of wings: one set for flying and the other to protect them.

BEETLE WINGS

BAD EYES

Beetles can't see very well. They find things using smell, sound, or by feeling vibrations. Our friend the dung beetle also uses the glow from the stars to find its way home.

BEETLE ENVIRONMENTS

Which of these beetles looks like it's in the right environment?

A: All 3...they live on all continents except for Antarctica.

Many beetles are armed with fierce-looking horns and pincers. The bombardier beetle creates its own mini explosion from its backside, firing out a boiling hot fluid at its would-be attackers!

LITTLE TOUGH GUYS

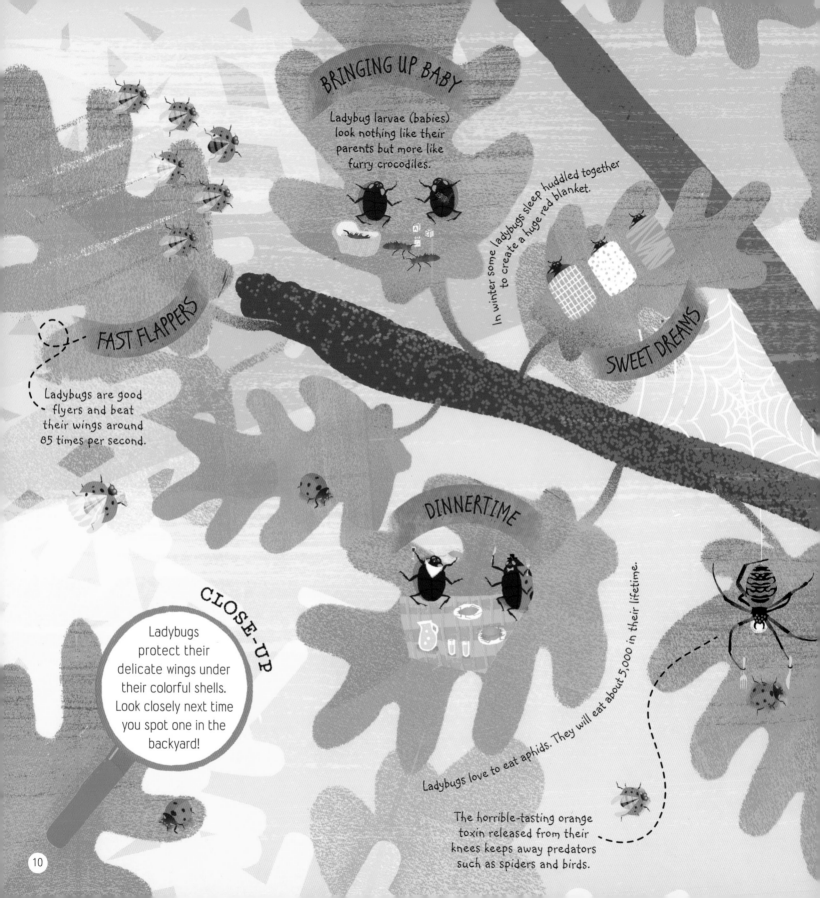

BRINGING UP BABY

Ladybug larvae (babies) look nothing like their parents but more like furry crocodiles.

In winter some ladybugs sleep huddled together to create a huge red blanket.

SWEET DREAMS

FAST FLAPPERS

Ladybugs are good flyers and beat their wings around 85 times per second.

DINNERTIME

CLOSE-UP

Ladybugs protect their delicate wings under their colorful shells. Look closely next time you spot one in the backyard!

Ladybugs love to eat aphids. They will eat about 5,000 in their lifetime.

The horrible-tasting orange toxin released from their knees keeps away predators such as spiders and birds.

10

LADYBUGS

Have you ever wondered why ladybugs are called ladybugs? Some say that they are named after the Virgin Mary after farmers prayed to her to protect their crops. Ladybugs came and ate all the pesky aphids, and the farmers exclaimed: "The Beetles of Our Lady!" So, you see, ladybugs are very useful insects because they eat pests and keep our farmers happy!

KNEE-JUICE PIT STOP

Ladybugs live in rotting logs, under leaves and rocks, and sometimes they sneak into people's houses.

Ladybugs' knees contain an orange fluid that they secrete when they're scared.

HOME SWEET HOME

In 1999 four ladybugs were sent to live in space on a NASA shuttle!

Eggs

Adult

Life Cycle

Larva (mini crocodiles)

Pupa (almost fully grown!)

LADYBUG LINE-UP

LUCKY CHARMS

Some people think ladybugs are good luck, can predict the weather, and even cure a toothache!

MYTH BUSTER

A common myth is that a ladybug's spots show its age. They don't—they are a reminder to predators that ladybugs don't taste very nice and are not good to eat. They can also tell you which of the 5,000 different species they belong to.

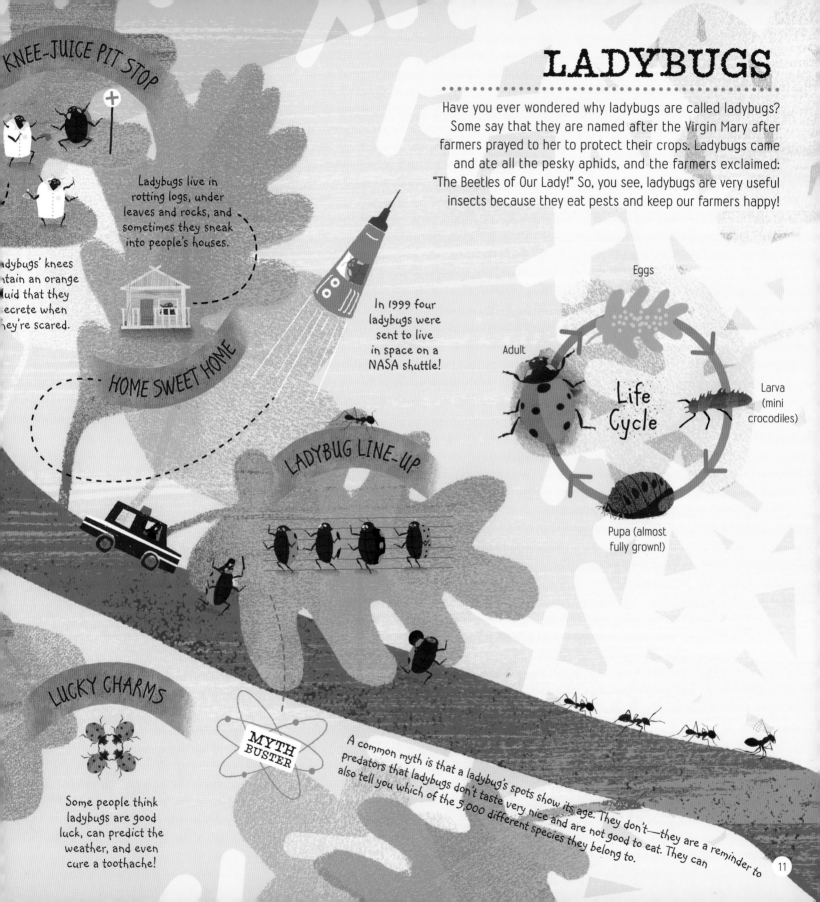

Worms tunnel in the ground mixing soil, which helps plants grow.

? ? ? ? ? DID YOU KNOW? ? ? ? ? ?

Worms don't have lungs, they breathe through their skin. The mucus that covers their skin helps them to breathe more easily. That's what makes them so slimy.

Worms have no arms and legs. Their bodies are covered in small bristles that they use to move and burrow.

Worm poo is full of nutrients and is great for the garden.

Worms come to the surface when it rains so they won't drown. That's the best time for you to go on a worm hunt!

NATURAL GARDENERS

WORM HUNT

Worms can eat their own weight in organic waste, soil, and minerals every day.

WASTE DISPOSAL EXPERTS

WORLD'S BIGGEST

MISSION
Why not start your own worm farm and watch them wiggle and tunnel their way through the soil?

The longest worm is the African giant earthworm, which can grow to nearly 23 feet long!

2 1 3

EARTHWORMS

Worms have been around for at least a billion years and are one of nature's most useful creatures. They have some pretty amazing tricks up their sleeve. They help plants grow, they can move without legs, and can even survive being cut in half! Find out why they are so good to have around in your garden and just why they are so slimy.

WORM PIE

Worms make a tasty treat for birds, toads, moles, beetles, and slugs.

When worms come to the surface they become vulnerable to predators.

MUTANT WORMS

Worms can have up to five hearts!

Life Cycle

Worms hatch from cocoons

Hatchlings

Worms can live between 4–8 years.

MYTH BUSTER

Many people think that if a worm is cut in half it becomes two worms. This is not true. Only the end with the head will survive.

WORMS EVERYWHERE

You can find a million worms in an acre of land.

BLIND AS A...WORM

Worms cannot hear or see. It's no wonder they bump into each other all the time!

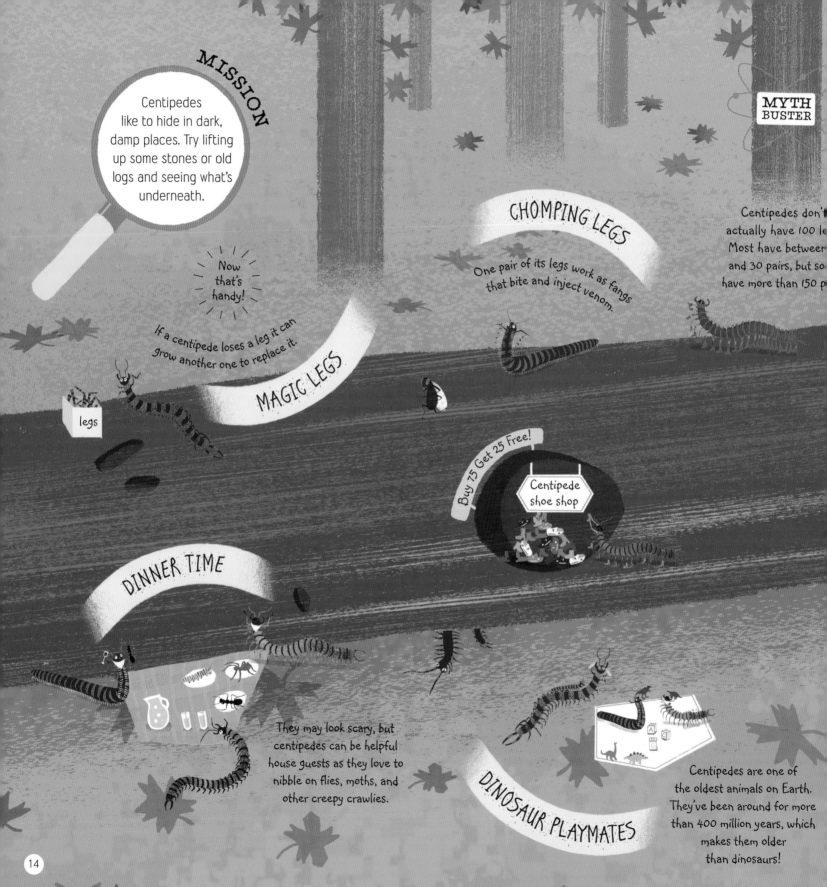

MISSION

Centipedes like to hide in dark, damp places. Try lifting up some stones or old logs and seeing what's underneath.

CHOMPING LEGS

One pair of its legs work as fangs that bite and inject venom.

Centipedes don't actually have 100 le Most have betweer and 30 pairs, but so have more than 150 p

Now that's handy!

If a centipede loses a leg it can grow another one to replace it.

MAGIC LEGS

legs

Buy 75 Get 25 Free!

Centipede shoe shop

DINNER TIME

They may look scary, but centipedes can be helpful house guests as they love to nibble on flies, moths, and other creepy crawlies.

DINOSAUR PLAYMATES

Centipedes are one of the oldest animals on Earth. They've been around for more than 400 million years, which makes them older than dinosaurs!

CENTIPEDES

Centipedes are, in fact, not insects! Like millipedes, they are called myriapods because they have long segmented bodies and far more than six legs. They love to live in dark and damp places, and are most often found in forests and woodland. However, you can sometimes find them creeping around the house, so look out!

To grow, they shed their skin, which is called molting. Every time they molt they sprout a new set of legs.

MOLTING

Life Cycle

Eggs

Nymph

Adult

Centipedes shed their skin as they grow

GLOBE TROTTERS

They're fast little critters!

QUICK MOVERS

All those legs help them scurry quickly up walls and across floors.

WHERE ARE MY GLASSES?

Centipedes can't see very well, so they use their antennae to feel their way around.

Centipedes can be found all over the world, from tropical rainforests to the Arctic circle.

A snail's eyes are on the tip of the tentacles on the top of its head. Get up close and watch them wiggle!

Snails make a tasty snack for birds!

Whenever danger is near, a snail can curl up in its shell to protect it from harm.

I'm not here!

Ssshh!

Baby snails are known to hitch a ride on the back of their moms!

MOBILE HOME

Snails carry around their homes—their shells—on their backs.

HIDE!

HITCH A RIDE

SLOW SNAIL RACE

Snails are some of the slowest animals in the whole world.

In the olden days, a broth made of snail mucus was used to cure sore throats.

SNAIL SLIME

Have you ever wondered why snails leave behind a trail of gooey slime?

It helps protect them from the surface they're traveling across and creates suction so they can move upside down.

Why not stage a snail race in your garden and see for yourself!

SNAIL SOUP

SNAILS

Snails might be one of the slowest creatures around, but they're actually very intriguing. They've been around much longer than we humans have, and they adapt very well to all environments. That's why you'll find snails all around the world and in your backyard, too! Have a look next time it rains and try not to step on them!

In many parts of the world snails are cooked and eaten as a delicacy.

Life Cycle

Eggs

Baby snail

Adult

As a snail grows its shell grows too

CHOMP CHOMP!

Snails scrape up their food using a spiky tongue, which can contain more than 14,000 teeth. No wonder they're so good at munching!

SUPER SNAIL STRENGTH

Snails are very strong. They can lift up to 10 times their own body weight.

Snails can't hear you. They don't even have ears!

MORNING!!!

Hmmm?

NO EARS HERE!

SNAIL OR SLUG?

Sometimes people get confused between snails and slugs.

A slug is like a snail without the shell.

See if you can find a spider spinning a web. Watch how it weaves its special trap and catches its unlucky prey.

Spider silk is stronger than steel!

Spiders build amazing silk webs to trap their prey.

Spiders can have up to eight eyes. This makes them experts at staring competitions!

WONDERFUL WEBS

The most common type of web is the orb web, like this one.

Spiders often make one web a day, so instead of wasting their old webs they eat them.

GOOD VIBRATIONS

Spiders don't have ears. They can "hear" the tiny vibrations of an insect coming closer through the hairs that cover their body.

SPIDER SOUP

Spiders can't chew or eat solids, so they liquify their prey into a soup that they suck.

Fly soup, ladybug smoothie, and organic beetle juice. Yum!

Some male spiders bring presents or perform a little dance to attract the female's attention. Others pluck their webs like a guitar.

FEARSOME FEMALES

Female spiders are often bigger than males. Sometimes these scary ladies eat their male suitors after they've mated. Gruesome!

8-LEGGED ROMANCE

18

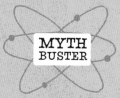

MYTH BUSTER

Spiders are not insects. They belong to a family called arachnids, which all have eight legs. Insects only have six legs, although sometimes their antennae look like legs. Now you can spot the difference!

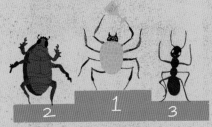

(Legs competition)

SPIDERS

Those scary looking beasts you find lurking around the house and backyard in fact lead very interesting lives. There are more than 43,000 different kinds of spiders in the world, and they range in size from ones the size of a pinhead to the dinner plate–size goliath bird-eating tarantula! They use their little fangs to inject venom into their prey, but luckily for us most spiders are harmless to humans.

Spiders lay their eggs in a silk sac.

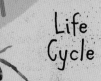

Life Cycle

Adult

Baby spiders hatch as spiderlings.

Spiders may not be able to fly, but they can balloon! Some small spiders and young spiderlings pull out their silk until the wind lifts them into the sky.

BALLOONING

Some spiders don't build webs at all. Instead they hide and chase their prey.

Boo

Arghh!

A nocturnal spider called the bolas spider uses its silk like a fishing line to catch moths flying past.

LET'S GO FISHING

MASTERS OF DISGUISE

Spiders are very good at disguises. The bird dung spider looks just like bird droppings. It even smells like it, too!

CLOSE-UP

Take a closer look at the fly's incredible compound eyes. Each eye contains thousands of tiny lenses!

Wheeee!!!

Flies are very good flyers. Not only do they fly very quickly...

...they can fly backward, hover, and spin!

STUNT PILOTS

ROMANTIC FLIES

"Fly me to the moon!"

Some male flies sing to female flies to attract their attention.

Flies taste with their feet, which are ten million times more sensitive to sugar than the human tongue.

FANCY FEET

Flies have hairy, sticky feet that allow them to walk upside down. Just like Spider-Man!

MAGGOTS

Maggots can be used to make cheese. Yum!

Maggots usually eat whatever they are born on. They love to eat and need to feed to become flies.

Baby flies are called maggots and can often be found on food or in garbage cans.

FLIES

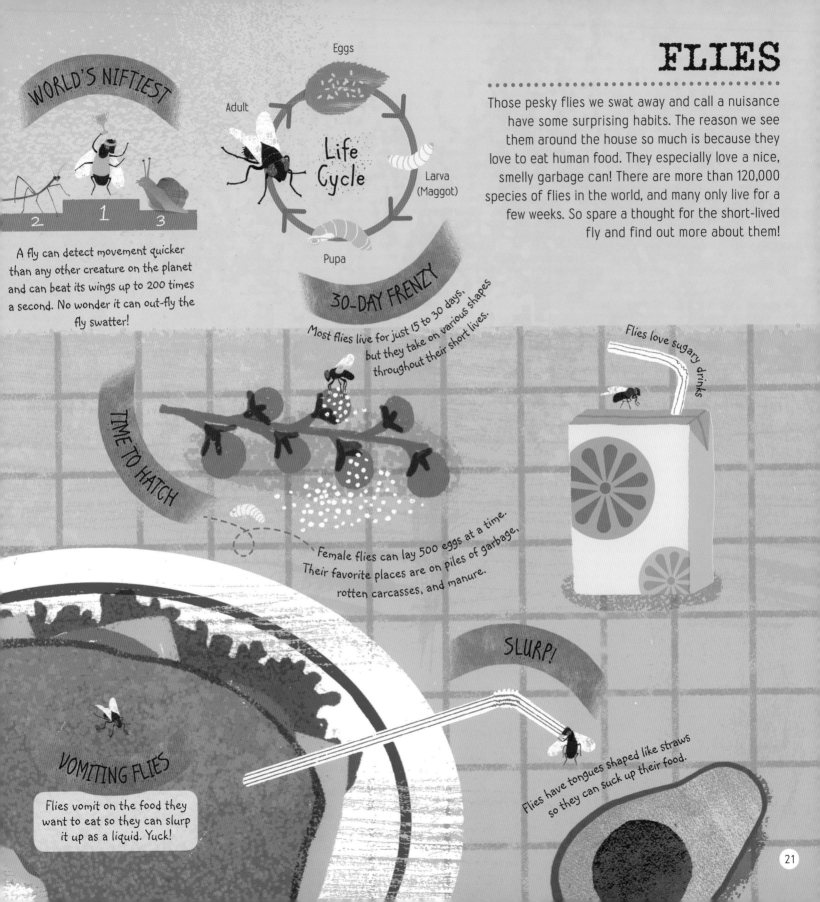

WORLD'S NIFTIEST

2 1 3

A fly can detect movement quicker than any other creature on the planet and can beat its wings up to 200 times a second. No wonder it can out-fly the fly swatter!

Life Cycle

Eggs

Adult

Larva (Maggot)

Pupa

Those pesky flies we swat away and call a nuisance have some surprising habits. The reason we see them around the house so much is because they love to eat human food. They especially love a nice, smelly garbage can! There are more than 120,000 species of flies in the world, and many only live for a few weeks. So spare a thought for the short-lived fly and find out more about them!

30-DAY FRENZY

Most flies live for just 15 to 30 days, but they take on various shapes throughout their short lives.

TIME TO HATCH

Female flies can lay 500 eggs at a time. Their favorite places are on piles of garbage, rotten carcasses, and manure.

Flies love sugary drinks

SLURP!

Flies have tongues shaped like straws so they can suck up their food.

VOMITING FLIES

Flies vomit on the food they want to eat so they can slurp it up as a liquid. Yuck!

An ant's skeleton is on the outside of its body instead of inside. This "exoskeleton" protects the ant like a suit of armor.

On guard!

KNIGHTS IN SHINING ARMOR

Left a bit!

TEAMWORK

Ants are great at teamwork. They can join together and turn themselves into a "raft" to escape big puddles, or climb on top of one another so they can reach up high.

They have to be careful though, predators such as anteaters love eating ants.

ANTEATER ALERT!

WORLD'S HEAVIEST

They may be tiny, but if you weighed all the ants in the world they would weigh more than all the humans.

JOIN THE ANT GYM

Ants can lift and carry things many times their own weight. If you were as strong as an ant you could lift a car above your head!

ANTS

They may be tiny, but ants are mighty insects! With super strength and speed, ants work together as a team to build and maintain their homes. Ants are social beasts and live in large groups called colonies, much like you live with your family. Next time you go outside, have a look at the ants and see if you can follow their trail!

CATERPILLAR HERDERS

Mooo!

Some ants herd caterpillars, just like a farmer herds cows. They take them out in the day to feed on leaves, then keep them safe in the nest at night. In return the ants "milk" the caterpillars for their delicious honeydew.

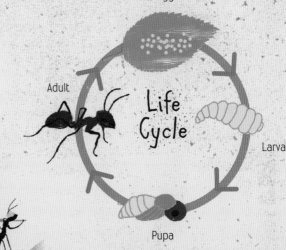

Eggs

Life Cycle

Adult

Larva

Pupa

AMAZING NESTS

Most ants build a nest to live in. Inside there are lots of rooms connected by tunnels. The rooms are used for different things, like storing food, sleeping, or as a nursery. There's even a special chamber just for the queen.

GIRL POWER

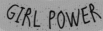

All worker, soldier, and queen ants are female. The male ants usually only live long enough to mate with the queen and then they die.

SPRING CLEANING

Ants are very clean and tidy. They even take their garbage out like we do.

TINY FARMERS

Ants have been farming even longer than humans. Leafcutter ants bring leaves back to their nest and grow fungi on them to feed the colony.

CHAMPIONSHIP RUNNERS

Ants have extra strong legs, so they can run really quickly. If you could run as fast for your size, you would be as fast as a racehorse!

AMAZING POLLINATORS

Bees fly from flower to flower, sipping nectar and collecting pollen.

Bees can tell each other where to find the best nectar by performing a special dance called a "waggle dance."

Turn left at the next daisy!

Past the greenhouse!

You can't miss it!

DANCING BEES

When they move to the next flower they leave some pollen behind. This helps the flower make new seeds and grow fruit like blackberries and strawberries.

MYTH BUSTER

"Bees die if they sting you." Not true! There are more than 20,000 species of bees, and only honeybees die after stinging.

HONEY MAKERS

The honeybee is the only insect that produces a food we can eat.

HELP SAVE THE BEES

Many fruits and vegetables would disappear if it weren't for bees. You can help save the bees by growing bee-friendly plants in your garden.

BEES

Bees are amazing! They live in colonies that are ruled over by a queen, and are essential to the environment because they help plants and flowers grow through a process called pollination. These busy little workers also produce something we humans can eat, honey!

MISSION

Next time you see a bee look for the little yellow sacs on its legs. They're filled with pollen the bee has collected from flowers.

When a bee looks at a flower it can see special little landing strips that guide it to the nectar.

WHAT'S THE BUZZ?

The bee beats its wings an amazing 200 times a second (that's fast!). This is what helps make their buzzing sound.

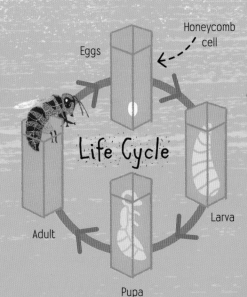

Life Cycle

Honeycomb cell

Eggs

Larva

Pupa

Adult

QUEEN BEE

Worker bees are all female and do most of the work, from collecting nectar to cleaning the hive and attending to the queen.

The queen bee lays ALL of the eggs in a hive. She is so busy laying eggs that she has no time for any chores.

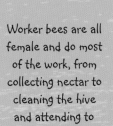

The "forager" bees take the nectar back to the hive in their special "honey stomachs," then pour it into honeycomb cells.

The "processor" bees fan the honeycomb by flapping their wings. This helps "dry out" the nectar and turn it into delicious honey.

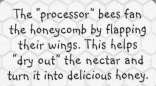

BUSY AS A BEE

Making honey doesn't come easy—to make a single jar of honey a hive of bees would need to visit 2 million flowers.

BUG DETECTIVE ACTIVITIES

Now that you know a little more about the weird and wonderful lives of bugs it's time to put your bug detective skills to the test. With your magnifying glass you can discover a world of activity that you've never seen before. So put on your boots and head into the backyard to see what you can find. Tread carefully and leave no leaf unturned!

GO ON A BUG HUNT!

Where to look
The best place to look is under things—leaves, stones, plant pots, and logs. Bugs also like to hang around flowers, trees, and plants. Remember, some bugs are very good at camouflage, so you'll need to look up close. Don't forget to be as quiet as you can so you don't scare them away, and be careful not to squish them!

Remember to set your newfound friends free after you've inspected them.

What you need
* Magnifying glass
* Glass or plastic jar
* A wooden spoon
* Notebook and pen

BUG DETECTIVE FINDINGS
Name of bug:

Where I found it:

Description:

Top Tip!
Bugs love sweet things. Try mashing up a bit of banana mixed with sugar, then spreading it onto a tree trunk. Wait a few hours then see what's turned up for dinner.

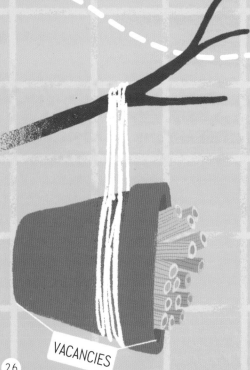

VACANCIES

MAKE A BEE HOTEL
Bee numbers are in decline, which is not just bad news for honey lovers. One in three mouthfuls we eat is the result of an insect pollinators' work, so dinnertime really would be boring without them (imagine no apples, strawberries, or tomatoes!). You can lend a hand by giving the bees somewhere to rest their weary wings and lay their eggs in the long winter months.

1. Bundle together some hollow plant stems like bamboo and Queen Anne's Lace.

2. Tie them together with some string.

3. Hang the hotel in a sunny, sheltered spot, at least 3 feet from the ground.

4. Now watch and see what drops by! As well as bee the odd ladybug and other insects may pop in.

5. Keep an eye out for the tiny mud doors coverin the entrance holes. This means a female bee has laid an egg inside.

WORM VS. SNAIL
Set up a race between these two slimy plodders and see who can out-slow the other! Which do you think will win?

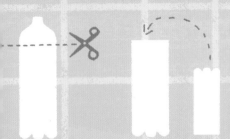

MAKE A WORM FARM

What better way to watch these wiggly creatures up close than to build your very own worm farm.

What you need
* Two clear plastic bottles (one big one, one small one)
* Sand
* Soil
* Leaves
* Vegetable peel

MAKE A LADYBUG

Turn a simple stone into your very own ladybug. Find a nice flat pebble, then paint on the colorful red shell and black spots (acrylic paint is best).

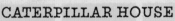

STEP 1 — Cut the tops off the plastic bottles (better still, ask a grown up!).

STEP 2 — Put the small bottle, upside down, inside the big bottle. This will make it easier for you to see the worms' trails.

STEP 3 — Alternate layers of sand, soil, and leaves, then top with some vegetable peel, coffee grounds. or tea leaves.

STEP 4 — WORM HUNT! Time to find your new tenants. Try digging in the soil just after it rains. Worms prefer things moist, so wet your hands before picking them up.

STEP 5 — Add the worms, then cover with some paper towel and secure with an elastic band to stop the worms wriggling away.

STEP 6 — Wrap a sheet of black paper around the bottle. Worms love the dark, and this will help them get settled in.

STEP 7 — Leave in a cool dark place for a couple of days (remember to water it every now and again so the worms don't get thirsty).

STEP 8 — Take off the black paper and watch the worms as they mix the soil, build tunnels, munch up the food, and even have babies!

Remember to set your worms free after a few days. The lovely fluffed up soil can be used in your garden to help the plants grow.

CATERPILLAR HOUSE

Make a comfy home for a caterpillar using an old egg carton. Find some nice green leaves for it to munch on, then add lots of soft moss and grass to make it nice and cozy.

BUG IDENTIFICATION GUIDE

Use this handy guide to figure out what's what in the bug world.

INSECTS have six legs, a body in three parts, and usually wings (beetles, ants, bees, and butterflies are all insects).

ARACHNIDS have eight legs and a body in one or two parts (spiders and scorpions).

MYRIAPODS have a head, segmented bodies, and lots and lots of legs (centipedes and millipedes).

ANNELIDS have long wriggly bodies in lots of segments, but no legs (the gardener's friend, the earthworm).

GASTROPODS have squishy bodies in one part and some have a coiled shell (snails and slugs).

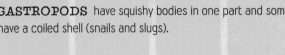

GLOSSARY

ABDOMEN
The main body (and back third) of the insect, where the reproductive and digestive organs can be found.

ANTENNA (OR ANTENNAE)
Long feelers that can be used to sense touch, heat, sound, smell, and taste.

ARTHROPODS
Animals that have a hard outer shell called an exoskeleton (see below). All insects, spiders, and centipedes are arthropods.

COCOON
A covering usually spun from silk that some insects (such as moth caterpillars) use to protect them at the "pupal" stage.

CHRYSALIS (OR CHRYSALIDES)
A moth or butterfly at the "pupal" stage of growth when it is turning into an adult and is enclosed in a hard case.

COMPOUND EYE
An eye consisting of a large number of individual lenses.

ELYTRA (OR FOREWINGS)
The hard, shell-like pair of wings on a beetle that protect a second pair of "flying wings" that sit underneath.

EXOSKELETON
A hard outer shell that supports and protects the soft parts of some animals.

HABITAT
The natural home of an animal or plant.

IMAGO
The name given to the fully grown adult insect after metamorphosis.

INVERTEBRATES
A creature without a backbone. All our friends in this book are invertebrates.

LARVA (OR LARVAE)
The young feeding stage of an insect that undergoes complete metamorphosis.

MANDIBLES
The chewing jaws of an insect.

METAMORPHOSIS
The changes that take place during an insect's life as it turns from a young animal to an adult.

MOLTING
When an insect sheds the outer covering of its body.

NYMPH
The young stage of an insect that undergoes incomplete metamorphosis. The nymph is usually a mini version of the adult except that its wings are not fully developed.

PROBOSCIS
The strawlike, sucking mouthparts on insects like flies, bees, and butterflies.

PUPA (OR PUPAE)
An insect in the non-feeding, transformation stage between the larva and the adult stages.

THORAX
The middle part of the insect body where the legs and wings (if they have them) can be found.

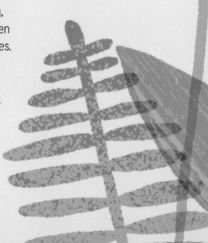